# ACE Your

*ACES and the Angry Employee*

Traci Shoblom

and Larry Pate

ImagineACES Productions, LLC
5111 Falcon Ave,
Long Beach, CA 90807
www.imagineaces.com

ISBN-13: 978-1984095350

ISBN-10: 1984095358

Printed in the United States of America

## Dedication

To those with the courage to let go of the life they planned so as to have the life that is waiting for them.

Traci & Larry

# Table of Contents

Part One: Phases One and Two

# Chapter One: Stuck!

"David! This is Leah. Are you almost here yet? Jim is on another rampage again and customers are literally starting to LEAVE the showroom. We can't keep letting him do this! We're losing business."

David Jenkins felt that familiar tightening in the pit of his stomach. *Great. I'm not even at work yet and the problems are already starting. It's gonna be another wonderful day, I can tell already.* "Yeah, Leah. I'm just a couple miles away. Do what you can to calm Jim down and I'll talk to him when I get in."

He almost felt like turning the car around and going back home. But, frankly, these days, home was not much better. Ever since Vanessa's parents moved into their "guest" room, things have been just as bad at home as at work. Vanessa keeps insisting that the only option is for Todd and Susie to live with them and it's causing a major strain on their marriage. It's even starting to affect the twins, Curt and Chris. "Daddy, Grandma keeps messing with our stuff. When are they going to leave?"

A blaring horn and shout, "Move it, buddy!" from behind him startled David out of his reverie. It was a good metaphor for how David felt in his life—stuck and not moving forward. *I seriously have no idea how what to do about all of this*, he mused as he started the last two miles to work. *Something has to change...*

***

"Jim, could you please come into my office?" David walked back from the showroom with the eyes of the entire staff, including Leah, following him. It was as if they were pleading, "Can't you do something about him?"

Jim Myer followed David into the small office in the back of the warehouse of Heirloom Furniture. His head was down and he didn't make eye contact with anyone. "David, you don't understand..."

"No, Jim. YOU don't understand! We have been friends since college. You're my best designer. Half the furniture in this place was designed by you! You are the most talented guy we have. But ever since your heart attack, things have changed. You know this. We've talked about this a dozen times. You can't just keep yelling at people."

"David, would you please just listen? That guy was challenging me on the materials we use. I couldn't just stand there and let him insult us. He even accused us of outsourcing to countries that use child labor! Was I supposed to just stand there and smile and agree with him?"

"Jim. This isn't about today. It's about all the days since you got sick. You were, as you acknowledge yourself, 'temperamental' before the heart attack. But since then, your anger issues have gotten even worse. Leah and the other employees are afraid to talk to you about anything because they never know when you're going to explode. Your working relationships are suffering. Even your work quality is starting to..."

"The quality of my work is FINE, David. You just said I'm your best designer. You know, this is sounding more and more like discrimination because of my illness. I can't believe you'd put a fifteen-year friendship on the line because some snivelly coworkers don't want to hear the truth about the quality of THEIR WORK and because I won't stand by and let idiots accuse us of using inferior materials and child labor. I'd think you'd be THANKING ME instead of blaming me.  This is BS, David. Total, BS."

The sound of David's office door slamming echoed through the warehouse. He could almost feel the eyes of everyone looking at him though the closed door. *Well, that went well, don't you think?*

Standing there in the aftermath of Jim's tirade, David's cellphone started to ring. He could tell from the ringtone that it was Vanessa. Sighing, he hit the "answer" button.

"David. You need to come home early. Dad is insisting on going to Home Depot and buying a new camping tent with his Social Security check. You know they don't even go camping anymore and he can't afford to be spending money on stuff they don't need. Mom and I are trying to talk to him but he won't listen. Curt and Chris are all excited to sleep in the new tent that Grandpa said he's buying and I don't know what to do. Can you please come home early and talk to Dad before he spends $200 he can't afford?"

"I'll do what I can, Vanessa. It's not even 10:00 am yet and things are already bad at work. I'll come home as soon as I can."

David put his head in his hands. *Talk about being stuck between a rock and a hard place!* Just then, he heard a knock on his office door. *Lord, please don't let it be Jim again...*

***

"David, can I come in?" It was Leah, peeking her head in the door.

"Sure Leah. Listen, thanks for letting me know about Jim this morning. I really don't know what to do about him."

"That's what I wanted to talk to you about." Leah pulled up a chair toward David's desk. "At work last month, my sister attended this workshop on decision making. Her company brought in these two consultants and they spent half a day teaching them about the kinds of traps that people fall into when they make decisions."

"I feel like I'm stuck in a trap, that's for sure."

"Well, Amy said that they taught her how to use this decision-making technique and she used it to figure out what to do about when to have a baby. They decided to go ahead and start trying now, by the way, which is really cool. But I was thinking that maybe you could use that decision making thing on the problem with Jim. She says it's called ACES and it's really easy to use. Do you want me to get the number of those consultants so that you could call them?"

David thought about it for a minute. On the one hand, he didn't really feel like unloading all of his problems on some stranger. On the other hand, this Jim situation wasn't getting any better on its own. Normally, he'd talk to Vanessa about it but with all the problems at home, he really can't talk to her about anything. "Sure. Why not? What do I have to lose?" As Leah went off to call her sister, David thought, *If this ACES thing can work on my problem with Jim, it can work on anything.*

# Chapter Two: The Meeting

"Dad, can I come with you?"

David turned and looked at Chris standing in the kitchen eating a bagel. "No, Chris. This is a business meeting."

"I won't be in the way, Dad. I promise. I just have to get out of here. Grandma says she wants to cut my hair! The last time she did that I ended up looking like one of the Three Stooges. Please, Dad!"

David sighed. "Chris, no. This is an important meeting and I need to concentrate. I'll tell your mom not to let Grandma cut your hair. We do need to get it cut, though. I'll take you and your brother to the barber tomorrow. We'll make sure you both look like Justin Bieber instead of the Three Stooges."

"Dad!"

David chuckled at that image as he walked out to the garage. Pulling out of the driveway, his mind started to wander ahead to the meeting. *I seriously doubt this guy is going to be able to help me with the Jim situation. This has been going on for months—years really. How can some decision-making process help solve THIS tough problem. But, it doesn't hurt to talk to the guy, right?*

***

"David Jenkins? Hi, I'm Larry Pate. Nice to meet you."

David extended his hand as he walked into a local coffee shop, Company Perks. "Hi Larry. Nice to meet you, too. My friend Leah and her sister speak highly of you." He was surprised at how warm and engaging Larry seemed to be. "Can I get you some coffee?"

"No, I've got some already. You go ahead and I'll wait for you here in this sitting area."

David collected his thoughts as he stood in line for his coffee. When he got back to the chairs and table, Larry had a notepad out.

"So, tell me a little bit about what's going on, David."

"Well, after I got my MBA, I started a custom-manufactured furniture business called Heirloom Furniture. We hand craft furniture for residences and businesses. Anyway, about a year into it, I hired my best friend from college, Jim Myer to work with me as my lead designer. He has a Master's in Fine Art and has always been, well, passionate. But it wasn't anything I couldn't handle—until about a year ago when Jim had a heart attack.

He was in the hospital for about a week and was off work for about six weeks. We were all really glad to see him come back to work. But when he got back, his personality seemed to get worse. He constantly snaps at the other employees and argues with everyone. We even had one person leave because she couldn't work with Jim anymore. He's defensive about the quality of his work—which has been slipping, by the way. And, now, he's started to go off on customers who come into the showroom! That's totally unacceptable!" David was starting to get upset as he was talking.  Pausing to compose himself, he took a deep breath.

Larry said, "It really sounds like a difficult situation, David. What have you done so far?"

"Well, I've tried to talk to Jim several times. He either gets defensive and angry at me, or promises to improve. But he doesn't! I am completely stuck as to what to do." David paused and took a sip of his coffee.

"I can imagine. I also imagine that this is spilling over into other areas of your life, too."

"It is! Things are terrible at home. I'm not sleeping well. I don't want to be at work and I don't want to be at home. Life sucks right now!" David managed a little laugh so that he didn't sound so pitiful to Larry.

Larry put down the notepad he'd been writing on. "David, whenever we feel stuck in making a decision, it's because we are falling into one or more 'decision traps.' And, we ALL do it at one time or another. I've got some stories I could tell you—that I tell in our workshops—of some bad decisions I've made that would shock you. It's a totally common thing. That's why my business partner and I started this business in the first place. Between the two of us, we've made just about every bad decision on the planet and we wanted to teach other people how to avoid making our mistakes!" Larry laughed a deep, resonant chuckle that put David at ease.

"Well THAT'S good to know. So, how do I get unstuck?"

"First, let me tell you a little bit about how people make decisions. Most of us don't even think about HOW we make decisions at all. In essence, making a decision is making a choice. It's a cognitive behavior, meaning that it's something you do mentally. And, each one of us has certain 'mental models' about how we see things, and those mental models influence the choices we make."

"I get it. It's like when we design a piece of furniture. The blueprint is the model that we use to see how the piece is going to turn out."

"Yes. And if you want to change how the furniture turns out, you have to change the blueprint. Well, when we have a decision to make, there are three activities that we do. They are intelligence gathering, design, and choice. Very similar, I imagine, to your furniture business."

"Yes!" David was enjoying this conversation.

"So, as I mentioned, there are some decision traps that we tend to fall into when we're making tough choices. There are ten of them, and I have a list of them here I'll give you so you can read more about them on your own. But some examples are giving disproportionate weight to the first information you receive, or favoring alternatives that perpetuate the existing situation, or making choices that justify previous, flawed choices."

David nodded. "It's like when my brother married the first girl he dated in college. We all told him he needed to date around a bit more first but he didn't want to hear it. Sure enough, it didn't last five years."

"Exactly. We fall into these traps because we make faulty assumptions about the situation. Or, we don't get clear on our priorities or values. We tend to think in either/or terms. 'Either I leave or I stay.' And many times we don't even think to ask 'What other information do I need?'"

"That's true. With the Jim situation I haven't even thought about what other information I might need. I'm only feeling stuck between not wanting to fire my friend and not losing any more customers or employees. So what do we do, then, to get out of these traps?"

"That's where The ACES Decision-Making Technique comes in. I developed it so that people could get unstuck and avoid falling into the traps."

"Why did you call it ACES? Did you come up with it in Vegas?" David chuckled as he took another sip of his now-cooled coffee.

"No, actually, I came up with it as I was teaching a university class. I was a professor before my business partner and I started our company. My students helped me create ACES more than 25 years ago and since then I've used it with literally thousands of people. It's called ACES because ACES is an acronym that stands for the steps in the process. They are Assumptions, Criteria, Evoked Set, and Search."

"Evoked what?"

"Evoked Set. It's an academic term for 'the list of options I'm currently considering.'"

"Oh, you mean like, 'Running away to Hawaii or jumping off a bridge?'" David laughed.

"Well, I hope not exactly that, but yeah." Larry smiled. "I'm going to ask them to warm up my coffee. Be right back."

As Larry walked up to the counter, David noticed that he was starting to feel better. *Maybe this ACES thing really can help with the Jim situation. Wouldn't that be great? At least ONE of my problems would be solved.*

Larry came back and sat down across from David, sipping his coffee. "Much better. I can't drink cold coffee at all. Unless it's supposed to be cold."

"So, Larry, do you think this ACES thing can work on my problem with Jim?"

"I know it can. I've seen it help hundreds of people in situations similar to yours. The vast majority of the problems we see are relationship problems—just like the one you are facing. It's important for you to understand, though. ACES doesn't SOLVE your problem. It just helps you reframe the situation so that you can see it differently and can come up with some other possible solutions. You'll end up with a plan to get additional information so that you CAN solve the problem. Of course, many times, going through ACES does solve the problem. But the value in ACES is in changing the mental model that frames the problem in the first place."

"Yeah, that makes sense. It's like ACES helps me recreate the blueprint so that the furniture turns out differently. So, how do I get started? Do I have to sign up for a workshop or something? Do you coach people one-on-one?"

Larry took off his glasses and leaned back in the chair. "You can do either one. Whichever you prefer. We do have workshops coming up. Or, we can work together just you and me."

"Let's do the coaching. I want to fit this around everything else I've got going on. My in-laws are living with me at the moment and, well, let's just say it's not good."

Larry chuckled. "Yeah, my business partner always says that leftovers and houseguests should be thrown out after four days. So, when do you want to meet next?"

David and Larry set up a time for the following Saturday to start working through ACES. After a handshake and goodbye, David walked out into the sunshine-filled parking lot feeling optimistic already.

Unfortunately, that good mood only lasted thirty seconds, as his cellphone rang. It was Todd, Vanessa's dad.

"David. Where are you? I thought we were going to Sears today to get the boys some new clothes. I can't wait to see them in matching outfits."

David groaned. His kids would kill him if he let Todd buy them matching outfits. *Well, at least I'm seeing improvement in ONE area of my life.*

\*\*\*

*Note: To see the list of Decision Traps that Larry gave David, see Appendix One.*

## Chapter Three: Assumptions

"Dad. We DID clean our room!" Curt was standing by the front door with a football in one hand and a bottle of water in the other. "Go look."

"I did look. I hardly consider shoving your stuff under the bed and in the closet 'cleaning' your room. Go get your brother and clean your room again." David could see his mother-in-law Susie sitting on the couch, leafing through a magazine and peering over it at him.

"You know, David, when Vanessa and Valerie were girls, we printed out their chores on a list. We never assumed that they knew what we meant when we told them to go clean their rooms."

Trying not to show his irritation, David said, "That's a good idea, Susie. Maybe we'll do that when I get back. I'm racing out the door to get to a meeting." David passed his sullen sons on his way out the front door. He reached out and mussed their hair with both hands. "Be back later, guys, and we can throw that ball around. Get that room clean!"

***

Once again, Larry was already in the seating area with his coffee when David arrived at Company Perks. They greeted and David went to order his coffee. Checking his phone while he waited, David discovered a text message from Leah. "Jim is at it again. Call when U can." David groaned.

"Pardon me, but this isn't what I ordered," David said after he took his first sip.

"You ordered a vanilla roast drip." The girl behind the counter gave David a blank stare.

"Yes, but this is sweet. Drip coffee isn't supposed to be sweet."

"Well, that's how we get it to taste like vanilla. We add syrup." Again, with the blank stare.

"But when your company sells this in the grocery store, it's not sweetened. It's just vanilla flavored coffee. I just assumed that since it's listed the same way on the board that you'd serve the same thing you sell in the market."

The girl at the counter was still staring blankly. "Nope. We can't sell that here. So we add syrup. Do you want me to make you something else?"

"No. It's fine."

David walked over to the seating area where Larry was and sat down. After some chit chat, David said, "I sure hope this works. I got another text from Leah just now that Jim is at it again in the showroom. I really don't want to fire him, but I'm starting to think I don't have another choice."

"Well, I'm sure that the ACES process will help you to see things differently. It really is effective at reframing things. Did you bring the four pieces of paper like I asked?"

David took out four blank sheets of paper. "Is this alright?"

"Yes, that's perfect. The ACES Decision-Making Technique is completed in four phases. The first phase is for you to make the worksheets. In the past, we've done it where we give the participants pre-printed worksheets. But, it's not really as effective. There's something about you making them yourself that starts to get your mind involved from the beginning. Do you have a pen?"

"Yes. And, I brought one for you, too. It's an Heirloom Furniture pen." David handed the pen to Larry.

"Hey, thank you! What a nice surprise. Okay, the first thing to do—Phase One—is to label the worksheets. At the top of each page, in the middle, you are going to write one of the letters of ACES. So, on the top of one, you write A. Another you write C. And so on." Larry looked on as David did as he was instructed.

"Like this?"

"Perfect. Okay, now, down the middle of the A, C, and E worksheets, you're going to draw a vertical line that divides the page in half. Don't do that on the S worksheet, though. The S worksheet is different."

David drew the lines. He felt kind of silly drawing lines on paper like this, but trusted Larry and his expertise. "Okay. Done."

"Now, at the top of the "S" worksheet, I want you to write out the problem you are facing." Larry leaned forward and took a sip of his coffee.

"You mean like, 'Should I fire Jim or not?'"

"No, that's not quite right. Firing Jim or not firing Jim are possible solutions to the problem. You want to phrase it like, 'What do I do about blank?'"

"Okay. So I write 'What do I do about Jim's anger issues at work?'" David waited for Larry to nod before writing it down. "All right. I'm done with that."

"Great. You've just finished Phase One of The ACES Decision-Making Technique! Have a great week." Larry had a gleam in his eyes and a smile. "I'm kidding, of course. Let's talk a little bit about assumptions before we go on to Phase Two. What do you know about assumptions?"

"Only that thing I was taught in school about how when we assume it makes an "ass" out of "u" and "me." David chuckled as that sounded like something one of his kids would say.

"Yes, I believe we've all been told that at one point or another. But the thing is, David, we are ALWAYS making assumptions about things. We couldn't live our lives without them. When you got into your car to drive here, you assumed it would start. When you walked in, you assumed that I would either be here or would be along shortly. We don't even think about our assumptions—we just make them."

"I never thought of it that way."

"Exactly! But what happens is that sometimes our assumptions are flawed. For example, I couldn't help but overhear your conversation at the counter there about your coffee. You assumed that because the company sells a product in the store by the same name as what they sell here in the coffee house that it would be the same coffee. That's a natural assumption, by the way. But it was a flawed assumption."

David took a sip of his overly sweet coffee and nodded. "Yes, that's exactly what happened."

"Of course we aren't suggesting that you go around challenging every assumption that you make all day long. But when you are stuck with a tough decision, challenging your assumptions can often help. Sometimes we are making flawed assumptions and we don't even know it!"

"So that's the second phase of the ACES process? Challenging my assumptions?"

"No. Actually, in order to challenge your assumptions, you have to IDENTIFY them first. Phase Two of ACES is getting your current view of the situation down on the left hand side of the worksheets. What I'm going to have you do is make a list on the left side of your "A" worksheet of all the assumptions you are making about the problem with Jim. Come up with as many assumptions as you can and list them on the left side of the "A" worksheet. Then, we'll meet in a couple of days and see what you've got. And, thanks again for the pen!"

"Sounds good, Larry. I think it's going to feel good to get all this out of my head and onto paper." The men shook hands and David packed up his things and headed out to the car. *Well, I better head over to the showroom and do some damage control with Jim before I go home to play ball with the kids.  I am definitely getting sick of this!*

*Note: To see David's worksheets for the ACES Decision-Making Technique, see Appendix Two.*

# Chapter Four: Criteria

David sat at his desk looking at the computer screen with his arms folded behind his head. His accountant, Jan, was right. Business was starting to suffer. David knew in his heart that this problem with Jim was the root of it. David was glad that Larry was coming by the warehouse today for a meeting. Maybe if Larry could meet Jim and Leah and everyone else, he might have some suggestions on what to do to improve the situation.

"David," Leah said, sticking her head through the slightly open office door. "We're going to lunch. Do you want us to bring anything back for you?"

"Thanks anyway, Leah. Vanessa packed me a lunch. Is everyone going?"

"Everyone except Jim. We asked if he wanted to go but he said no."

"Not surprising. Well, have a good lunch. See you in an hour or so."

David saw Jim sitting at his desk as everyone else went out to lunch. Jim was staring out the window watching them all get into Leah's minivan. He could tell that the situation was as hard on Jim as it was on everyone else. David got up from his desk and walked into the warehouse.

"Hey Jim. How's it going?"

Jim quickly looked away from the window and down at some furniture orders. "Fine, David. I'm fine."

"You want to come in my office for a bit? Vanessa packed two sandwiches for me again. She must think I'm too skinny, or something." David chuckled as he patted his slightly rounded belly. "I think I've got a couple of beers in the minifridge, too, if you want."

Jim looked at David and paused for a moment before saying, "Sure, Dave. It's been awhile since we just sat and talked over a beer. Let's not talk about work, though, okay?"

"Sounds good, man." As David watched Jim walk ahead of him into his office, he remembered how good his friendship with Jim was at one point. They had been best friends through some of the most difficult times in David's life. He couldn't help but wonder, *Will Jim and I ever be that close again?*

***

"Hey David. That guy Larry is here. Do you want me to send him in?"

"Sure, Leah. Thank you. And if I haven't told you lately, thanks for everything. I really appreciate having you around here." David smiled.

"Yeah, yeah. Say it in my paycheck." Leah smiled back as she went to go send Larry into David's office.

David stood to greet Larry has he walked into the office. "Welcome to Heirloom Furniture!"

"Thanks, David. What a great facility you have here. Would it be possible to get a quick tour of the place before we get started? I'd love to see how custom furniture is created."

"Of course!" David was proud of the business he'd created and was thrilled that Larry cared enough about him to want to see the process from start to finish.

****

"I am really impressed, David," said Larry as he sat down in the office. "I admire fine craftsmanship and you certainly focus on that here. Do you see this watch I'm wearing? It's the same watch that the astronauts wore in the Apollo program. I bought it in the late 1960s and it's the only watch I have ever worn. There's no need to get something else when you have the best. And, clearly, you focus on creating the best."

David smiled at the compliment. "Well, we certainly try."

"So, how did it go with the left side of the A worksheet? Were you able to list all of your assumptions?"

"Yes. And actually I thought of another one this afternoon that I added to the list. Jim and I had lunch today and it was great. We just talked about old times and laughed like friends. I realized that one of the assumptions I am making is that letting him go will end our friendship. That's part of why I'm so stuck. My friendship with Jim is really important to me and I don't want it to end."

"That is a perfect segue into the next step in the ACES process. It's the left side of the "C" worksheet— criteria. Criteria are 'What is important to me in this situation?' So, one of your criteria items is, "Keeping my friendship with Jim." What else is important to you?"

"Well, the business is starting to lose money. So, stopping that is important to me. And keeping the high standards of quality in our work. I won't compromise on that. Also, having a positive work environment. And happy customers." These seemed obvious to David.

"Good! Those are the things that you'll write on the left side of the C worksheet. Think of as many things as you can. Don't worry if they seem obvious or if some of the items seem to conflict with other ones. We're just getting your current framework down." Larry stood up.

"Okay. I can do that. Do you want to meet at Company Perks again on Saturday?"

"Sounds good, David. Traci, my business partner, and I have a workshop we're running in the afternoon, but I can meet with you in the morning. Say, 11:00? You know… I just had an idea. Would you like to come to the workshop? It's from 1:00-5:00 and it might help you to get a better picture of where we are going with ACES."

"I'd like that, Larry. Let me check with Vanessa and see if we have any plans. I don't think we do, but you know how wives are…" David chuckled.

"Yes, David. I certainly do," Larry replied with a twinkle in his eyes. "Give me a call and let me know about the workshop. Regardless, I'll see you Saturday morning with your C worksheet."

# Chapter Five: Evoked What?

"Hey! You beat me here this time!" Larry was laughing as he walked into Company Perks.

"I had to get here half an hour early to do it!" David grinned. He was really starting to enjoy these meetings. "Go ahead and grab your coffee. And make sure it's hot! I know that coffee being hot is on your list of criteria items."

Larry smiled. "You're learning! Good!"

David sat back down and pulled out his worksheets. *I wonder what kinds of problems everyone else will be having at the ACES workshop today?*

Larry came back and sat down. "How did it go?"

"This was my favorite part of ACES so far. I started to really get clear on what I value—what's important to me. It's so easy to get sucked into the negative side of a problem that you lose focus on what matters to you." He handed Larry the C worksheet.

Larry looked it over and said, "I'm glad. The C worksheet is one of the most crucial parts of the process. After all, what you value and what I value could be completely different. It's the C worksheet that allows a person to make a choice based on his or her own values and not a choice that is dictated by what someone else wants."

"Okay, so what's next? I know my assumptions and I know what's important to me? How do I get from here to solving my problem?"

"Well, again, we are still just identifying your current frame of the situation. So, the last step in doing that is to write down your evoked set."

"My evoked what?"

"Your evoked set. It's a term that means 'the options you're currently considering.' So, what are the options you've been considering?"

"Pretty much just two options—keep Jim and hope for the best or fire Jim. That's why I'm stuck. I don't like either of those options."

"I can imagine that. You know, in our work with ACES, more often than not, people only have two items on the left side of their E worksheet. 'Stay or go.' 'Take this job or that job.' So, you're in good company here. In fact, ACES was created for just this kind of problem. There are four types of problem situations." Larry got out a piece of paper and drew a square with eight boxes. "The problems are either simple or complex, routine or novel, real or imaginary, and structured or ill-structured. You'll hear me go more into detail about this at the workshop today. But the problem you've got with Jim is what we call 'ill-structured.' You're not choosing from a predetermined set of alternatives. It's not 'Do I buy a Porsche or a Mercedes?' It's not as structured as that."

Looking out the window at Larry's car, David said, "I can see which choice you made in that problem situation, there, Larry. I'd love to have a problem like that."

Larry looked down modestly and said, "Yeah. I'm a bit of a car aficionado."

"Well, your passion for craftsmanship is clear from your choice of cars, that's for sure." David appreciated that Larry seemed to value excellence as much as he did. "Okay, so I just write down my options on the E worksheet? That should take about one minute. What then? I start on the S worksheet?"

"No, not yet. Once you've finished the left sides of the A, C, and E worksheets, you're done with Phase Two of ACES. Let's head out to the workshop and meet again in a few days to start on Phase Three."

"Sounds good. Can we take your car?"

"Ha ha. Yes, we can. I'll tell you more about the history of the car on the way."

****

Following Larry into the meeting room at a local hotel, David noted that the room was filled with, probably, twenty-five people ranging in age from their thirties to their sixties. *All of these people are stuck with a problem?* David thought. *I guess I'm not the only one.* He was looking forward to learning more about ACES and how it can help other people solve their problems too.

A short blonde woman with a huge smile walked up to them and extended her hand. "You must be David. Larry mentioned you'd be joining us today. I'm Traci, Larry's business partner. It's so nice to meet you. Larry told me about his tour of your warehouse. I'd love to come see it myself some day. Please, sit anywhere you'd like."

As Larry went up to the front of the room to set up, David and Traci walked over to a round table that had a couple of people sitting at it. "Who are all these people? Do they all know each other?" David didn't want to intrude.

"No, no. This is a workshop that is open to the public. Larry and I do two kinds of workshops—ones for the public and ones inside of companies. The ones inside of companies deal with interpersonal issues at work. Like employee problems or tough management challenges. The ones for the public deal with more personal problems. Sometimes we hold workshops for health related problems—that's my specialty. Other times, like today, we tackle family problems like parenting, marriage, and in-laws. Oh! Larry's calling me. We better get started. There's some water over there if you'd like some." With that, Traci walked up to the front of the room.

*Family problems! Boy am I in the right place today.* For the first time, David started to wonder if ACES could help him with the problem with Vanessa and her parents.

For the next several hours, David immersed himself in the workshop. He learned more about the types of problems people face, the traps that people fall into when making choices, and what goes into making an effective decision. He learned how to avoid decision traps and what the components of ACES are. Of course, he was already familiar with some of it through his coaching with Larry. But being in a group setting and listening to other people's questions, challenges, and stories really added depth to David's understanding of ACES.

At his table, David met a woman whose problem was, "What do I do about my son's behavior problems?" The man next to him said his problem was "What do I do about spending more time with my kids now that I don't live with them?" Next to him was a couple whose problem was, "What do we do about getting over the affair?" David was surprised and honored with the openness people had in sharing their toughest problems. The workshop was really a "safe" place for people to work through an issue that was clearly very important to them.

After Larry finished giving his overview of ACES, Traci said, "Okay, in a few minutes we are going to take a break and then when we come back we'll start to work through the ACES process on the problem you just identified."

Right then, David's phone vibrated, alerting him to a text message that had come in.

"David. You need to come home. Mom and Dad are packing to leave. They say they don't want to stay where they aren't wanted. Please! Come quickly!"

David's heart sank. He didn't want to leave the workshop but he couldn't just let Todd and Susie leave on bad terms. He packed up his things and went to talk to Larry. "Something urgent has come up at home and I have to go."

"Oh no! I hope everything's alright."

"Yes. Nothing life-threatening. This drama with my in-laws is about to hit the fan and I need to get home and deal with it. We're on for Wednesday at Company Perks, right?"

"Yes. And call me if you need me, David. I care."

*He really does. I can tell,* David thought as he called Leah to come pick him up and take him back to his car.

# Part Two: Phases Three and Four

## Chapter Six: Reversing Assumptions

"David! I'm so glad you're home!" It was clear that Vanessa had been crying as she rushed to meet David's car.

"What happened? Everything seemed fine when I left this morning."

"It started with the boys. They came to me and were complaining again how hard it is having Grandma and Grandpa around all the time. I told them that it's hard on all of us, but that I don't really see another choice. There's nowhere else for them to go. Well, it turns out that Mom was right in the next room and she overheard everything. She said, 'Well, if we're being such a burden, we'll just go.' And then she went to go tell Dad and now they're packing. I don't know what to do, David. I feel so stuck. I don't want them to leave like this but I don't want Curt and Chris to be miserable. What do we do?"

David took Vanessa in his arms and kissed the top of her head. "We'll figure something out. I promise. Let's go talk to Mom and Dad and get them to stay for awhile until we figure this thing out."

David and Larry arrived at Company Perks at the same time. "This is getting to be a race to see who can get here first," David said as he walked through the door Larry was holding open for him.

After they got their coffees, Larry asked, "Is everything okay at home?"

"Yeah, things are a little better now. Vanessa and I talked to Todd and Susie and I told them that I'm learning this process called ACES and that it might be able to help us solve this problem. I asked them if they would stay until the end of the month to give me time to finish our coaching and then we'll use ACES to figure out what to do about their living situation. After a lot of tears between Vanessa and Susie, they agreed to stay. So, I bought some time on that problem, anyway."

"Good. I'm glad. I'm also glad that you're seeing the value of ACES for different kinds of problems. Once we've worked through it for your problem with Jim, it should be easier for you to use it on your problem with Todd and Susie. Are you ready for Phase Three of ACES?"

"Yes, I am. I was bummed that I had to leave the workshop early. I wanted to see how the rest of ACES works."

"Well, the next step in ACES is to reverse the assumptions that you listed on your "A" worksheet."

David pulled out the worksheet and his Heirloom Furniture pen.

"By the way, thanks again for the pen. I use it all the time," Larry said. "Okay, so for every assumption you listed, you reverse it by adding the word "not" or taking away the word "not " in the sentence. So, what's your first assumption?"

"My first assumption was that Jim is the best designer in town."

"Okay so the reverse of that assumption is that Jim is NOT the best designer in town. Write that down on the right side of the paper, next to the first assumption."

David did as instructed. "Okay, my next one is that Jim would not be able to get another job. So the reverse of that is that Jim WOULD be able to get another job, right?"

"Right! Now you're going to do this for every assumption you listed. This is the trickiest part of ACES for a lot of people. They get confused on what the reverse assumption is. So for example, if one assumption is "Jim is a great designer," the reverse assumption isn't "Jim is a terrible designer." That's not the reverse assumption. The reverse assumption is Jim is NOT a great designer. There are a lot of things in between being a great designer and a terrible designer. So that's why you only change one word by adding in or taking away the word "not." Let's try one more so that we can be sure you've got the concept."

"Let's do the one I realized that day you came in. 'Letting Jim go would end the friendship.' That becomes 'Letting Jim go would NOT end the friendship.' Hey! I never thought about that before. What if we could become just friends again instead of the stress of being boss/employee? Wow. That never even occurred to me."

Larry's eyes lit up as he smiled. "Exactly! That's what ACES does. It helps you see things you never thought of before. So the next thing is to ask yourself, "Under what conditions would letting Jim go NOT end our friendship?"

David thought about it for a minute. "Well, maybe if Jim wasn't happy with his job either. You know, I never even asked him if he still likes working here."

"Well, then that's your first item for the 'S' worksheet. The 'S' worksheet is a list of things you need to find out. It's the information you need to "search" for in order to solve your problem."

David pulled out the "S" worksheet. At the top was written the problem "What do I do about Jim's anger problems at work?" On the sheet he wrote, "Ask Jim if he's happy working at Heirloom Furniture."

"This is amazing, Larry. I can't believe I never thought of that before."

"That's the key, David. Reverse your assumptions and then ask yourself, 'Under what conditions would the reversed assumption be true?'"

"Wow. Okay. I'm going to do that. You want to have our next meeting at my house? I'd like for Vanessa to meet you."

"I'd like that. Thank you."

David told Larry he'd talk to Vanessa about a specific day and time and get back to him. As he was walking back to his car, David felt happy for the first time in months. *This is going to work. I can solve this problem with Jim!*

# Chapter Seven: Weighting Criteria

"Larry, this is my wife Vanessa, our sons Curt and Chris, and Vanessa's parents Todd and Susie. And, that over there is our dog Chip."

Larry shook everyone's hands and said, "It's nice to meet you all. David has told me so much about you."

"Dad just told us about you this morning," Chris said, with a mischievous grin on his face.

"Christopher!" Vanessa said, embarrassed.

Larry laughed. "No worries, Chris. I'm glad that your dad doesn't bring his work home with him."

"Come on boys. We'd better be going. That newfangled 3D movie we're seeing starts in half an hour." Todd shook Larry's hand again and said, "It was nice to meet ya."

Susie gave Larry a polite hug as Todd, Susie, and the boys headed out for the afternoon.

"Would you like some coffee, Larry?" Vanessa offered.

"I would, thank you."

"Make sure it's nice and hot, Vanessa. No lukewarm coffee around here." David winked at Vanessa. "She makes great coffee. Let's go sit in the living room."

As Vanessa was making the coffee, David pulled out the worksheets. "Man. I have to tell you. It was a real experience reversing those assumptions. I never realized that I was looking at things through such a narrow lens before. It would be like designing a piece of furniture and only thinking that I could use one or two different kinds of materials. It was so limiting!"

"I'm glad you found it valuable. It really is such a simple, yet powerful exercise to help us identify flawed assumptions."

"So I know from the workshop that the next step is to rank order my criteria in terms of importance."

"Not quite. You don't rank order them. You weight them."

"What's the difference?" David asked.

Just then, Vanessa came in with the coffee. "Is it okay if Vanessa stays?" David asked.

"Of course!" After everyone got their coffee, Larry continued. "The difference is that rank ordering forces the criterion items into an order. 'This one is more important than that one.' Weighting them looks at each one on its own merit. You can have more than one criterion item that is weighted a ten, for example."

"Oh! I see. So, how do I do it?"

"Well, first you go through each of your criterion items, and on a scale from zero to ten, with ten being very important and zero being not important at all, rate each item based on how important it is to you. What's the first one you have listed?"

"I want a peaceful workplace."

"Okay. How important is that to you?"

"I'd give it an eight."

"Okay, what's next?"

"That I want to keep the friendship with Jim."

"What's the weight on that one?"

"A ten. Definitely a ten. The next one is that I don't want to spend any more money on a salary if I have to replace Jim. He's working for less than market value now. It would cost me more to replace him. That was one of my assumptions. Although checking that out is on my 'S' worksheet. But anyway, not increasing my payroll is on my list of criteria. I'd give than one a 4."

David, Larry, and Vanessa went through each one of the items on the list. After, Larry said, "Okay, the next step is to reverse the weighting."

"What do you mean? I weighted them according to how important they are to me."

"True. But to get you outside your current frame of thinking, you want to imagine what it would be like if the item were more or less important to you than you thought. So, go through each item on the list and weight them all either a zero or a ten. All the high weighted items become a zero and all the low weighted items become a ten."

"Okay, so a peaceful workplace would become a zero?"

"Yes. And then ask yourself, 'Under what conditions would having a peaceful workplace be totally unimportant to me?'"

Vanessa spoke up. "Remember when we were in college and you worked for that startup company? That place was anything BUT peaceful. And you loved it!"

"That's right! Remember the all-nighters we pulled before deadlines? That was some crazy fun right there. Yeah, I guess maybe a peaceful workplace isn't as important to me as I thought."

"Good! You're thinking. That's good. What's next?"

"Keeping my friendship with Jim. That becomes a zero?"

"Yes. Under what conditions would keeping your friendship with Jim become completely unimportant?"

"I guess if he hit on my wife or something."

Vanessa laughed. "Yeah right. Jim's the most ethical guy I know, other than you, David. No way. That would never happen."

"So it would take something pretty extreme to make Jim's friendship unimportant to you."

"Yeah. I guess I never really realized how important our friendship was until I started going through this. That has to stay a ten."

Over the next twenty minutes, David, Larry, and Vanessa went through each item on the "C" worksheet and reversed the weights to either a zero or a ten.

As David was walking Larry to the door, he said, "I can't believe how much that process helped me. I am totally clear on what matters to me now. This ACES thing is amazing."

"I'm really glad it's working for you, David. I can honestly say that it's helped thousands of people get unstuck from their toughest problems. We are on the home stretch now! I'll see you in a couple of days at Company Perks. Meanwhile, take a look at your "E" worksheet and see if you can think of any new possible solutions to your problem."

"Sounds good, Larry. And, thank you. Thank you for everything."

# Chapter Eight: Evoked Set

David increased the speed he was running at on the treadmill to 7.7. He was no racer by any means, but David's workouts had become much stronger since he started using ACES. *It's funny,* David thought, *I'm using ACES in my mind all the time now. Even at the gym. When I think I can't go any faster, I start to challenge the assumption and think maybe I CAN go faster. This ACES thing is permeating my brain.*

David saw Larry walk into the juice bar at the gym, right on time. He got off the treadmill and, after grabbing a sanitizer wipe, greeted Larry. "Thanks for agreeing to meet here instead of Company Perks. I've got a meeting with Jim scheduled before work today and I wanted to get a quick workout in before the meeting."

"No problem. I'm actually a member of this gym, too. I'm meeting my friend Tom for a game of racquetball after our meeting. So, it worked out perfectly!"

David pulled out his "E" worksheet from his gym bag. "Well, I was able to come up with a couple of more options for the "E" worksheet. I remember you saying at the workshop that the items on the "E" worksheet in

Phase Three are "variations on the theme." So, one of my original "E" items was to fire Jim. Well, I started to think, 'What if Jim isn't happy working here and I HELPED him find another job?' It's not FIRING him; it's helping a friend. Of course that depends on what he says today when I ask him if he's happy working here."

"Great! That's great. What else?"

"Well, another one of my original items was 'Keep Jim and hope for the best.' A variation on that theme would be, maybe, to let Jim work from home on his computer. This way he would be out of the workplace and not getting agitated by customers and could focus on being a designer only. So I put on my "S" worksheet to talk to Jim about that."

"Fantastic. You're really getting this, David. I'm proud of you."

"Thank you." David felt strangely proud that Larry was proud of him. "Another item I came up with is to see if maybe Jim might want to get some coaching to help him deal with his chronic illness. I remember Traci telling me that her specialty is health issues. Maybe ACES would help Jim do a better job of dealing with his illness."

Larry laughed heartily and leaned back in his chair. "David, you are an excellent student. All of these are great ideas. You've put them on your "S" worksheet, right?"

"Yes." He pulled out the worksheet. "On here is 'Talk to Jim about if he's happy at work,' 'Talk to Jim to see about working from home,' "Talk to Jim about us finding him a different job,' and 'Talk to Jim about getting coaching from Traci.' Then, depending on what happens in my talk with Jim this morning, then other stuff will go on my 'S' worksheet. Like 'Find some job leads for Jim,' or 'Talk to Traci about coaching Jim.' But the first step is my talk with Jim."

"Good, good. You've really grasped the process. Do you have any questions for me at this point?"

"Yes. I do. I'm thinking of getting a new car and I was wondering if I should get a Porsche or a Mercedes?"

Larry laughed and said, "That depends on your wife, my friend..."

After agreeing to call Larry later that afternoon with the outcome of his meeting with Jim, the two men parted ways.

# Chapter Eight: Search

"Jim. Come on in and sit down." David glanced at the clock. *8:30—he's right on time.* David noticed that Jim looked a little nervous. *He probably thinks he's going to get fired.*

"Jim. First off, I want you to know that I didn't call you in to fire you. That's not what this meeting is about." David saw Jim take a deep breath and visibly relax.

"Good. I'm glad to hear that. Why am I here, then? Am I getting a raise?"

David smiled, "Well, not exactly, although I wish I could give us all raises. No, it's this. Jim, you and I have been friends since college. I'd even call you my best friend. When you had your heart attack—well, it felt like I was about to lose a brother. And, then when you came back to work and things got so hard... well, it was like losing you all over again."

Jim looked away, choked up with emotion as he said, "Yeah. It's been tough."

"Well, I've been working through this process called ACES with a consultant, and..."

"You talked to some consultant about me?" Jim's eyes flared with anger. "Great. That's just great." Jim sat back stiffly in his chair.

"Jim, listen. I want to save our friendship. You matter to me! And I could see that it was going down the toilet. This ACES thing made me realize that our friendship is very important to me. More important to me than us working together. I brought you in here today so that I could listen to what YOU really want. I want to know if you even want to be working here any more. Is this what you want to be doing?"

Jim sat in silence, thinking, for a minute. Softly, he answered, "I've been thinking about that a lot lately. I'm kind of burned out on designing furniture. But I don't know what else I could do. I'm too sick to change careers at this point. And my wife would kill me if I left my job."

"Do you KNOW that? Have you asked her? You see, that's the thing I learned with this ACES technique. Sometimes we make assumptions about things and don't even question them. Every thing you just said to me is an assumption. Maybe they are flawed assumptions."

Jim got defensive again. "So you're saying my thinking is flawed? Is that it? That I'm not right in the head?"

"No, Jim. I'm not saying that at all. I'm doing it too. I've got this problem at home with Vanessa and Todd and Susie and I'm stuck. So I'm going to use this ACES thing to get unstuck. All I'm saying is that if you're feeling stuck working here because you think you're too sick or you can't do anything else or that Karen wouldn't like it, then maybe take a look at those assumptions. Check them out. Like I'm doing right now with you."

Jim looked David straight in the eyes, paused a moment, and said, "I wouldn't be letting you down if I left?"

David said, "No, man. You'd be letting me down if you stayed and it ruined our friendship. I can hire another designer. Not as talented as you, for sure, but I think we can manage."

Jim smiled. "Well. Let me talk to Karen. Let me think about all of this. I walked in here thinking I was getting fired. My head is kind of spinning. Where did you hear about this ACES thing anyway? Did you sneak off to Vegas and not tell anyone?"

David chuckled. "I wish. No, Leah's sister went to a workshop with that Larry Pate guy that was in here a couple of weeks ago. He's the one who created ACES and I've been working with him on it for the past few weeks.

Not only about you and this situation but also about the thing with Vanessa. I even went to one of the workshops."

Jim seemed interested. "Hmmm. Maybe this ACES thing could help me? I feel kind of weird talking to a stranger about my problems though. I'm not a therapy kind of guy."

David laughed. "And I am? No, it's not like that. It was more like a professor friend teaching me how to solve problems. Not hugging and sharing our feelings. I'll give you his number and maybe you can just meet him for coffee. You've already met him here, anyway."

"Yeah. What do I have to lose, right?"

"Right! Look, Jim. I'm really glad we had this talk. I can tell that you haven't been happy for awhile now and I really want to help. If staying here is what you want, then we can make it work. But, if you're ready for a change and a new direction, I want to help you do it. After all, you're the guy who knows all my college secrets. Gotta keep you happy!"

"That's right. What happens in college should stay in college…"

Just then, Leah arrived. "Hey, you two. Did somebody call a breakfast meeting and not tell me?"

Jim smiled at her as he walked past, "Yeah. David says we're all getting raises."

# Chapter Nine: Bringing it Home

"Should we save some of this pizza for the boys?" Susie asked as she sat down at the dinner table.

"No, they've gone over to Liam's house to spend the night. Anna says that they're going to order pizza and play Minecraft all night. Besides, they don't like the Artisan pizza we're having" Vanessa said.

David sat down with Vanessa, Todd, and Susie and said, "I'm glad that the boys are gone for the night. Remember a couple of weeks ago when you both were ready to pack up and move and I asked you to wait? Well, I thought we could talk about it now...maybe use that ACES thing I learned."

"Well, I'm not sure that some tool you learned can help us with our situation, but it can't hurt to try," Todd said as he put a piece of pizza on his plate.

"Thanks, Dad. I appreciate it," Vanessa said.

David got out four pieces of paper, and walked them through the ACES Decision-Making Technique. Over the next couple of hours, they created the worksheets, defined the problem, and identified their Assumptions, Criteria, and Evoked Set. Then, they reversed their Assumptions, weighted and reverse weighted the Criteria, and expanded the Evoked Set. They filled in the Search worksheet with things they needed to discover in order to answer the question "What do we do about Todd and Susie's living arrangement?"

After dinner, they went into David's home office and had a Skype meeting with Larry and showed him the worksheets to make sure they'd done it right.

"David, Vanessa, Todd, and Susie... you guys have done a great job using ACES. How are you feeling about it?"

Todd answered first. "Well, I wasn't sure how this thing was gonna work. I mean, I'm old school. We didn't work through our problems on paper. We just sucked it up and dealt. But I could see that us living here is too hard on Susie and Vanessa." He put his arm around his wife.

It was Vanessa's turn. "We love having you here, Mom and Dad. But you're too young to spend the rest of your life doing nothing. I like the ideas we came up with on the "E" worksheet. Larry, we are going to check out this cool retirement community near my sister Valerie. It's not an old folks home at all. Instead, they have camping trips and karaoke nights. And because Mom and Dad have lived in California their whole lives they might be eligible for a discounted rate. So, that's what we're going to check out from the 'S' worksheet."

Susie said, "My best friend Cathy moved into one of those communities in Texas. She's always telling me about the fun trips they take. Last year they all went on an Alaskan Cruise! I could get used to that!"

Larry then said, "David. You've been pretty quiet there. What are you thinking?"

David paused. He took a deep breath and said, "I'm thinking that I'm really happy that I listened to Leah and called you. I was feeling so stuck before and my life was such a mess—no offense Mom and Dad."

They laughed and said, simultaneously, "None taken."

"But by using the ACES technique I went from being hopeless to hopeful. I really think that it's going to work out for everyone. I'm really just feeling grateful.

"I am very glad that you found ACES useful," Larry said. "Now, I just have one favor to ask of you."

"Yes. Anything. What is it?"

"Pay it forward. Get the word out. Tell people about ACES and how it helped you. This isn't about me or getting my name out. It's about helping people—all kinds of people—learn how to make better decisions in their lives. I didn't create ACES to get rich or famous. I created it because I know that if a person can learn to make choices that are in alignment with their values, they will make better decisions. And that is what leads to happiness. As Albert Einstein said, 'The important thing is to never stop questioning.'

# Epilogue

"David! Over here!" Jim's wife Karen was waving at him from a few rows over. "I've saved your seats."

David and Vanessa walked over to where Karen was standing. "Thank you so much for inviting us."

"Are you kidding? It's because of you that Jim is getting his degree in Computer Aided Design in the first place. There's no way you could miss his graduation. He's worked so hard the past two years for this. I'm so proud of him. He's so proud of himself!"

The voice over the loudspeaker announced, "Ladies and Gentlemen, please take your seats. The Commencement will begin in a few minutes.

Two hours later, David, Vanessa, Jim, and Karen were sitting around the table at The Cheesecake Factory. "I'd like to propose a toast to my best friend Jim." Everyone raised their glasses.

"Here's to a man who wasn't afraid to challenge the assumption that life ends after a heart attack. Here's to a man with the courage to take a new direction in his life. Here's to my friend Jim."

"Hear Hear!"

Jim raised his glass next. "And, here's to my friend David. A man who didn't give up on me or our friendship. Thank you."

Just then, Vanessa's cellphone rang. "It's my mom. Do you mind if I take it?"

"No, go ahead. We're about to break out the hankies and start hugging now anyway," Jim joked.

***

"Mom? Mom? I can barely hear you! Vanessa stood out in the parking lot of the restaurant. "Mom? Where are you?"

"We're at the top of Pike's Peak in Colorado! We took the Cog Railway up to the top. Remember I told you that everyone was taking a trip here?"

Vanessa did remember but couldn't keep her parents' travel schedule straight. Ever since they moved to the Third Act Retirement Community, Todd and Susie had been so busy that Vanessa barely heard from them.

"It's so beautiful up here. You and David really need to bring the kids up here."

"We will, Mom. Are you coming home for Thanksgiving? The boys miss you."

"Absolutely! I have a whole suitcase of mementos for them from our travels. What's that Todd? Oh! I have to go. We're taking a group photo. I love you sweetheart. See you soon."

Vanessa smiled into the phone. "You, too Mom."

Walking back to the table, she slid into the booth next to David. "Who'd have figured that ACES thing would completely change the lives of so many people for the better? Jim and Karen... Mom and Dad... and us..."

David looked at his wife and his best friends and smiled. "So, guys. I'm thinking of getting a new car..."

# Important Terms

Assumptions: Your working beliefs about the decision situations.

Criteria: Your priorities. What matters to you in the decision situation.

Evoked Set: The set of options you're considering for solving the problem.

Decision Making: The process of choosing from among alternatives (not dependent on achieving desired outcomes).

Decision Traps: A form of cognitive bias that causes us to make poor decisions.

Porsche: A German sports car, often regarded as the finest automobile on the road.

Reverse Assumption: The process of inserting or removing the word "not" to/from an assumption.

Search: A list of necessary action steps for getting "unstuck" on tough problems.

Weight: A numerical value given to identify an item's importance.

# Appendix One: Decision Traps

1) Plunging in – This is just like it sounds. You make a decision without fully gathering information or thinking the outcome through. And, you often come to regret it!

2) Frame blindness – This is when we are focused on the wrong problem because of the way you are framing the situation. One example would be a company that is focused on developing a new and improved DVD player, when in reality fewer and fewer people are using DVDs.

3) Lack of Frame control - Failing to consciously define the problem in more ways than one or being unduly influenced by others.

4) Overconfidence in our judgment - Failing to collect key factual information because we are too sure of our assumptions and opinions.

5) Shortsighted shortcuts - Relying inappropriately on "rules of thumb" such as implicitly trusting the most

readily available information or anchoring too much on convenient facts.

6) Shooting from the hip – This, too, is just like it sounds. It's making decisions based on the belief that we can keep all of the relevant information in our heads instead of using a systematic process to evaluate the different options.

7) Group failure - Assuming that with many smart people involved, good choices will follow automatically and therefore failing to manage the group decision-making process.

8) Fooling ourselves about feedback – We've all fallen victim to this at one point or another. We either don't believe what someone tells us because we don't want to hear it and so we convince ourselves that the feedback is wrong, or we believe false feedback because it's in agreement with what we want to hear. This can cause us to search and search for feedback, until we find what we want to hear, regardless of how reliable the source.

9) Not keeping track - Assuming that experience will make its lessons available automatically, and therefore failing to keep systematic records to track the results of your decisions and failing to analyze these results in ways that reveal their key lessons.

10) Failure to audit our decision process – This is when we don't think about HOW we are making decisions.

# Appendix Two: The ACES Decision-Making Technique

**Phase 1**
- Prepare worksheets

**Phase 2**
- Identify the present frame for viewing the problem

**Phase 3**
- Generate a new frame for viewing the problem

**Phase 4**
- Identify action steps for solving the problem

# Appendix Three: The ACES Worksheets

# A

| Current Assumptions | Reverse Assumptions |
| --- | --- |

# C

| What do you want? | Weight? | Revised? |
| --- | --- | --- |
| | | |

# E

| Options | Expanded Set of Options |

# S

Issue at Hand:  What do I do about _____?

Action Steps (Things to find out)

Notes

Made in the USA
San Bernardino, CA
05 February 2018